In the World I Love
You are perfect.

J. W. Christian

Copyrights © 2024 by J.W. Christian
All rights reserved.

Table of Content

Introduction ("In the World, I Love, you are perfect.") 1
Enduring Thoughts 3
"In the World I Love." 4
The Lord Has Given You another Chance to Love Again 7
Vision 8
Colorful Roses 9
Never ending love 14
Sinking love from a drowning heart: 27
I waited on you. 32
Broken with Love 43
If I had you? 44
Besides Loving You Forever 46
Missing you like yesterday. 48
Just a thread 50
The Lord Gave Me the Strength 52
The Inspiration of Love 54
Dreams and Roses are one. 55
So Much Love Between Us 58
Un-Substituted Love 60
Reconnecting 62
O tell me, my beloved, ... 63
And she spoke. 65
A Thousand Kisses 67
Relationships 69
Excellent Times between Us 70
The Lord, Feel your shame. 72
I Will Love You Always 74
Inside Forgiveness 76
A Love I Can Believe In 78
My Morning Dew 80
Last Thoughts 83

INTRODUCTION
("In the World, I Love, you are perfect.")

I see the moon has no problem smiling when you are around. I agree with the sun and its method of shining. I understand why the stars want to shine at night.

I can feel the elements of your soul shouting out the windows of joy. Life is a pretty sight to see when the heart is looking through the window of love. I cannot think of anything else that would replace what my heart is feeling. I would cross the seven seas to see your smiling face. I will not quench what I feel inside because you gave me light in dark places. I would think at night, and the world around me would light up. I would climb the highest mountain and jump from an airplane without a parachute to prove my love to you.

I would change the months of the year; I would name them all after you. To be around you is worth a thousand pictures over a fireplace. Your love is worth all the stars that surround heaven. Loving you is like waking up next to a star that fell out of heaven. Your love is a present under a tree that brings me joy year-round.

The sun rises because love has everything to do with you; your heartbeat, smile, and energy put a heartbeat into orbit. Your love is everything that holds merit that creates a cross walk between day and night. From a distance, I can see the rising and falling of each heartbeat that speaks with ten thousand tongues of your love.

If I lived another thousand years, I would count it all joy. "In the world I Love, you are perfect". You are the light that my heart desires. Your love is the joy that brought me through the storm. "In the world I love, you are perfect."

Enduring Thoughts

I lay by the fireplace with my ears glued to your past voice, waiting for your call. Like a broken man waiting for the phone to ring or a text to come through, but days has passed, and my mind played tricks on me; I know you are never going to awaken my heart, but I live with the hope that is you would one day.
"My heart was feeling what my mind was thinking, and it came true." The sun came up, and the moon took flight.
"You are not alone; somebody is experiencing what you are going through or been through."
"Great love comes as a package with great benefits with no boundaries."
"You hold the key to your success, your heart, soul and mind" is the lineup performer that will bring you goodness and laughter.
"We are the creator of our luggage that we carry around," Just unpack it.
"Stop killing your heart; it genuinely loves you."
"Love for one another will work if two souls are walking as one."
"Investing time in your heart will be an invaluable source that will become your greatest investment and the endless resources that will abide with you."

"In the World I Love."

The earth, sun, moon, and all its surrounding planets would be our stepping stones into heaven.
In the world I love, I can only think of you and the Happiness that I found in you.
Things will never be the same.
You are completely under my skin.
So much part of me that I cannot breathe without your love.
This world as I know it would be impossible to live in without you.
My heartbeat would run out of time and stop beating.
I would be unhappy for the rest of my life, and I would never be a winner. I will never experience Happiness.
I will never break through my loneliness.
I know how pain and hurt feel.
Because I am living it
Crying all day and night would be my result. My tears would flow like a river into a stream of sorrow.
I would have stopped breathing if you would have told me so.
In the world I love. You are it for me.
I see no life without you.
Without your Happiness, I would never be. My world would be nothing but a circle of faults.
A thousand-pound missile exploding in the open sea.
My heart would reach its limit and burst into midair.
There will never be another me without you. You created this life as I know it. You gave my existence new hope.

I would never experience another moment of Happiness without you.
Life may as well skip me and move to another side of the world.
I would never be any good to anyone, not even myself.
When I am near you, I can breathe and take my next breath.
My world without you would just be me living without purpose.
I refuse to let my mind wander; I would not have it any other way if you were not in my life.
If I take a vacation, I would be alone.
It would not be worth it for me to live and not have you by my side.
I have been in this world alone before, so I know how it feels to be lonesome.
If I cannot wake up next to you
I may as well close my eyes and sleep forever
If I am living a thousand years from now
For all the fish in the ocean and sea
All the piles of gold and silver on earth. From the bottom of the sea
To the width of the ocean to its depth
I would be nothing without you.
If you add up all the miles around the earth.
The distance to the moon and back would be endless thoughts of you.
For all the steps, I cannot count.
For all the numbers, I cannot repeat or recall.
My love will remain alive for you. Time is a reminder.
That I would be mindless without you, all the seasons would turn into one, and I would live a cold life.

Darkness would prevail,
And light would take a back seat.
Your absence, minus your presence, would be my darkest hour.
Without you, I may as well be blind and crazy that way, I will not remember you and the way it was.
Your love and heartbeat kept giving me a reason to live with desire.
My world would cave in without you. The desire within my heart is like passion of love reaching out from me. I will simply demise without you.
If I could not see you and touch you, my life would be sad and gloom
You may as well take my life.
I would not have any reason to live on. My life would be worthless and empty. I would be just an empty jar sitting on the shelf. I will never give up on us.
"In the world I love."
There is no me without you.
There is no you without me.
You are my ride-or-die.

The Lord Has Given You another Chance to Love Again

Do not give up because someone chooses not to love you.
In His hands, in my hands, in your hands
Our love for each other existence

Vision

Crying with the pain of missing you like flowing water into the ocean. Like flowing water down a scream. My tears are not helping me go over you. The vision is clear: there is nothing more I can do or add to my heartbreak to get you to come home again. I cannot reach into heaven and pull you back down. The Lord's provision is a great provider, but for the moment, I am crying but not cried out. There are few more tears left, just maybe, just maybe one day, I will get over missing you.

COLORFUL ROSES

You are not what they say you are.
For all the years of love that skipped you
Today is a new day for love to be.
Where the heart can breathe again
Where the sun is still rising
Where your heart can freely beat
Where your heart can rest in peace
And find a new path to follow.
Down creeks and across brooks
Like a flower on the side of a hill

Reaching the open sky
Outside the limit of time
Where rivers and evening speak
From the garden of rose where eyes met
Just beneath the dust, they came to be.
Were sand and soil playing dirt?
Where your tears fall from heaven
Where beauty comes in distinct colors
Like the shade of the sun going down
Reflecting off the ocean floor
Like a diamond in the ruff in the hands of its maker
You are my colorful rose.
Like a spark from the heart to ignite love through the eyes
of pearls, rubies, emeralds.
Color lines make up our heartbeat.
Like a rose of colors
I can only speak about what I feel.
A thousand miles of eyes
Pushing through challenging times to get here.
Losing friends and loved ones along the way.
And the morning still came.
But you never gave up your dream.
You kept pushing forward.
Amid our heart
Love spring from below
We held on and kept moving in harmony.
And create a world of our own.

In thirty-one poems
Falling seasons of tears
We came to know what love is.
We both had a desire to push for more.
With the light reflecting from the ocean bay
We created memories and felt each other's growth.
We looked at each other with an open heart.
And sometimes life still hurts.
We never want to experience longings again.
From the shadows, we grew
With different shades of gray
That gave us hope that love will always be.
Like rising and setting of the evening sun.
A thousand dreams with heavy thoughts
In thirty-one poems
Because we held each other down for so long.
Colors can blend into the soil of darkness.
Becoming a miracle for light to travel
From the clouds of gray lifted one's eyes
In the colors between misty grey and brown
Eyes can be open to feeling the rays of the sun.
Forever beaming down and pushing forward
Brass, silver, and gold like optic metals
Black and white are colors that create gray.
That holds the secret for love ingredients.
Like a heart that is full of energy
Pushing upward and through to fulfill its desire.

Like a heartbeat that is constantly giving
Bursting through and reaching for the sky
Like rainbows, light-reflecting through a prism
From the soil, it knew.
Love surrounds the tip of its borders.
Facing the sun, smiling with the morning dew
A rose with a trademark of beauty and destiny
Blossoming with a sparkle of living love
Dedicated to each step that is stairway to heaven.
Forever outlining the borders of touch
Forever cannot seize time, and time cannot slip away.
With the sun sitting behind it
Increasing the smile on our face
The wind was not enough to push our love over.
Speaking to the moon by night
Spreading love to other continents
We could not go a day without each other.
Showing love and spreading love
Where space and time look alike
Between us, crying took place.
Flowing from heaven like open clouds
With the sky wide open
Where angels refuse to stop crying
In thirty-one poems
If forgotten, take away our memory, we have nothing.
To remember is to have love always.
In the eyes of others, we will always be.

We set the standard that even the blind can see.
We gave hope that a broken heart would mend.
We both see the morning light as the sunrise.
In our heart, we will always be each other's rose.
Our garden will be a creativity of love.
Helping others understand their journey.
Stem from a heart that lives on the passion of love.
A colorful rose

Never ending love

Before the stars were born
Before it all came to be
Our past and present body language spoke freely.
In a message that only the heart understood
Our hearts stood at the gate of time.
We held space in our hands.
Our smile creates its beginning.

For we held the key to our dreams
Holding on to a moment.
If the Lord gave us another thousand years
We will start the beginning all over again.
And lived another ten thousand years.
You are the one thing that triggered a faithful heart to beat.
In time never ending our love started a new beginning
We stood close to the shore with the sun shining.
Playing with the tides as the ocean roll in
We can do this a thousand times.
And watch love goes back and forth.
We do not need anyone else around.
As we made a wish on a falling star
Listening to the thunder rolling
As the whispering wind channeling across the open ocean
Pushing against the seashore bank
We read each other's mind with open desire.
There is nothing left but
Our love for each other
Where the end is no more
Where the beginning of love is never-ending
As I am rethinking my whole life
And watch time unfold.
We hold the key to each other's thoughts.
That would make our life come alive.
To watch the sun rise and set.
And give way to a new heartbeat.

Inside each other, we feel each other's pain.
We would watch the ocean tides.
Rushing in and out to shore
Claiming the old and bringing in the new
I saw our love riding the tides of time.
Pushing and holding back the current
Washing away any footprints in the sand
Giving us a fresh start
Where we once stood before this
We look back and smile.
For we know, we started it all
Our last two worlds started to collide.
Creating a new before and after day?
We had to say good-bye to back then.
You were not around to make me smile.
Sometimes, our heart fails to breathe.
We experience Happiness in a crazy way.
That kept our hopes and dreams alive.
Not leaving behind memories so long ago
Looping back to events from the past
Thinking back over the years,
It is easy to feel sentimental.
About the trivial things we let slip through.
But it is good to look back and feel good.
About the remarkable people we became.
Love puts beauty in every day.
Your eyes match the sunrise.

The warmth of your arms wrapped around me.
The joy of memories keeps the sun unfolding.
Not holding dreams at bay.
But keeping them alive.
Creating never-ending love
The older I got I would watch the sunset.
The more I thought about what matters to me.
My mind continually comes back to you.
What would my life be like without you?
So many false starts and setbacks
And things that once seemed impossible.
You gave me the strength to move forward.
Now, they no longer make the list.
What matters to me now?
Is the two of us—sharing our lives.
Reliving and believing in each other
Like the stars in place and the moon shining forever
Like memories and pictures are to dreams
This life with you and the moment we shared.
Seems like a perfect time to celebrate.
Your love and my love with the joy of each other
Holding hands and walking on the beach in the sand
With each step with the sand peeping between our toes
Not looking over our shoulder for tomorrow is today.
And all of yesterday is our memories that we hold so dear.
Without a look in your direction and, you the same
We would have missed each other, and what a shame.

Life would have been empty.
If we did not help each other breathe.
Our love taught us how to take our next breath.
About never-ending love
I unfolded time and put it in a bottle.
Our love will float across the seven seas.
Leaving the doors open
With instructions for a new foundation
Our heart begins to build.
My heart yearns for you and always will.
You gave the family a name that was everlasting.
Gifts that you can never retire or let go of
You stood tall, never blowing in the wind.
You brought a kindness that kept the heart beating.
A matching wave that jolts our world
Like a written note, we kept making history.
Creating a life that would be to this day no end.
Never erasing time, just adding to it
No lucky number in the lottery of life
Just a blessing gift of having each other's love.
A nurturing soul that turns into a beautiful bliss
Where time off will smile
Where space and room are glue
Where a little heartfelt gave purpose
Where love stood solo and spread its love ashore
Where time hung out with the beginning
Where a heartbeat understood what love is

Where our hearts were young once
We lived to pass those days into now.
Where our heart still beat the same for each other
Still seeing each other with a smile
Ten thousand words cannot explain or express.
A thorough change has come about.
Years rolled by me, I never expected.
Reaching in the distance so afar
I am not surprised by your love.
I saw that years ago the first time we hugged.
I was always aware of your beauty.
That kept time at bay.
I knew the world was changing,
but for you, time stood still
I put you first. I never felt last.
You have opened my heart to breathe.
Lifetime in a capsule
I kept to myself until you found me.
A day I thought would never be.
A moment where dreams can live again.
Along with all the things I felt inside.
Along with all the things, I still feel.
Open my soul to love you.
With never-ending love
To my heart that beat, I do remember
To my love that lived, I cannot contain.
To me, you have always been that friend.

That I always wanted
That never failed me but kept me holding on.
How much you meant to me.
I am trying to let you know.
Our glimpse of time was like a rainbow.
That is waiting for its moment to shine.
To be a promise keeper
In the presence of the Lord that you may see
That the Lord never forsakes us
Our journey took us around the world.
Memories and moments we hold so dear.
There are no special times like the present.
No wonderful memories than to remember.
We both have those birthdays that keep coming.
Each day brought something new to us.
That never grew old to us.
I will chase the clouds down.
And squeeze them so tight.
That they will cry tears of joy
For all the years I have loved you
Sitting on the edge of time with pretty wings
Speaking openly will all the stars.
I know it will take a while.
If I sleep a thousand years
And life passed me by
My heart will desire you.
My hopes are in you and with each thought.

I would be mist not to add my loving heart.
Beyond what I see and know
Heaven is near in loving you.
I cannot get enough of your love.
You have reminded me of goodness.
Where the path I am following.
Can be a wonderful door to open.
I feel that way when I am around you.
I know you have always been there for me.
Like a flower that is blossoming
We made beautiful memories.
Love we both can always cherish.
In feeling the way I do
I cannot speak without you.
My focus is all about you.
I understand you and what you have been through.
I see the best of you in your worst times.
Loving you is to love who you became.
Just the mention of your name
Bring joy to my soul.
A compassion that is not all about me
Awaken the stars to shine in their weakest hour.
Like the moon brighten up the night
We both have those precious moments.
That holds time together like glue.
The glance of your love makes the world go round.
I continue to love you without change.

I treat you with riches of my grace.
Every moment in constant care
A flame of love spring from my heart
The season rises and changes.
But my love for you withstood.
The test of time
About never-ending love
Through your strength, I can go on and on
No rest for me
My thoughts and love are about you.
I know tomorrow, one way or another, will come.
In your arms, I will wake up and start anew.
For yesterday was my promise
And today, I am living that promise.
Tomorrow will be a better day.
For the rest of my life, I will have you.
I can talk about the rain, sleet, and snow.
I can speak about the changing seasons.
I can open my eyes and wonder.
But with you, all things are possible
I see and feel the presence of your touch.
Every living moment with you is graceful.
I stop making wishes; I know hope by its name.
A bright and shining star you are.
My resolutions with you
For a reason unknown, our love borderline on time
I know why; I love the energy we are giving off.

No words can express what I feel.
The actual thoughts that are still teaching me how to live
I would never have made it this far without you.
I see how you were there for me.
That comes alive, tilling from the soil of love.
Nor can it express the affection that love feels.
The gladness and Happiness that it brought.
To meet the morning sun after the morning dew as come
What is so cool about you is your whispers are sweet?
You do so much for others that heaven noticed.
Something so smooth about you that my heart cries
That filled the lens of my eyes, that gladness flow with tears.
I am willing to share all of me, but my thoughts are speechless.
Love takes the words of a dear friend and never says I am sorry.
But opened their arms to hold and embrace them with love.
Their embracement makes them more substantial,
And you are their strength.
I see the miracle in your eyes and the smile it awakens.
You became majestic that was never-ending.
Never all about me but never-ending love
I cannot list the thousands of hours I hurt before you.
I promise to forget but you gave me forgiving power.
The past will never be with you again.

For you have a glance in the past and awaken the future
That love can live and always be, without a doubt, love.
Others could see the joy that you had, but I experience it firsthand.
The universe knows by now what love is because of you.
For you have set the example of what can be and to come
So, I am saying this to tell you our love will never, never end.
For beyond tomorrow, the future and I will always be.
Just knowing that we once loved is enough to keep the world turning.
Our love is more vital than a thousand seas put together as one.
I must prepare to leave now, but my love will remain.
The morning after will awaken with sadness.
The warmth of your love will still be present with me.
The times we have shared will continue to blossom.
And friends will see the stars dancing once again.
And they will know we once lived.
In times like this, it is hard to find the words that best convey.
Our deepest thoughts and sympathy one must feel.
For life and love will speak for us in volume
For we are an example that reference superhero
We will think warm thoughts that make the blood flow.
For the Lord is our shepherd and I shall not want, I fear no evil.

Let our memories warm our heart for the rest of our life.
For you have so much to love and be love and shared love
You have filled the hearts of so many and touched so many others.
Today is indeed remarkable, for it belongs to you and always will.
With the blessing and pleasant memories and short hour had dawn the morning.
Bright with joy and songs of the heart awaken the flower to come forth.
Budding from the soil and reaching toward heaven, a glimpse of you smiling
For we know this day would always be a beautiful day to behold
What our love did today will be effective for others.
They can trust and believe in one another again.
What we are today and tomorrow will always be strong
For we had each other's to hold on to and stand close to and lean on
Our life together had blossomed a new day to begin.
And that part of us that still live on will never cease to be.
For our love stood the test of time and weathered the storm
What remains is our commitment to love and show others that love.
Can live, and you can still believe in
About never-ending love

Where you can overcome and have no fear of standing alone
That the Lord sees your worth and rewards you with a crown of victory
Now you know the Lord was watching from above.
For you became the glory of His love
Because you showed others how to love
From the opening of your heart until your last breath
You showed honesty, kindness, and generosity.
That makes heaven your home where love still flows.

Sinking love from a drowning heart:

The morning before dawn
The night's turns and twists had awakened alone.
Floodgates of a thousand nights had rushed the shore.
I could remember the night before.
I had no energy to vibrate.
I was struggling and suffering to fight back.
Sinking love from a drowning heart
My life was in a bad place.
I could not see what was coming around the corner.
I was standing on the second floor.
Now, I am having second thoughts.

I been searching for a diamond in the rough
To shine and never lose it lust.
Now I am on the third floor.
I cannot see the sun rising.
There is a sinking heart feeling inside.
Under the ocean, tears
Reaching for the shore
Just one step away from an island floor
I woke up from this nightmare.
Only to find out I was in a deep sleep.
I just want you to know.
I want to make something new for you.
Start my life over and never look back.
But how can I?
When I know I have a deep desire for you
Rolling over and touching you is not possible anymore.
Life had lost its purpose for me.
So, I need to turn the page.
I can only think about it.
What can I do about it?
Whispering sweet nothings in your ear
Is not keeping you unharmed.
Telling you, you are my morning air.
Waking up without you had been devastating.
Knowing we can never love like that again?
Knowing we can never touch like that again?
I cannot dream without sleeping.

Living without you would be impossible.
There are times I refused to live on
I know how it feels to have a sinking heart.
I know how it feels getting the last drop.
Going down for the last count
Sinking in the middle of an ocean tide
Looking at the ocean floor
I thought our life would last forever.
You can see I am still calling your name.
You can tell I am still holding on to you.
Everything about you is still real to me.
You did not throw me a lifeline.
I start to sink with a broken heart.
Slowly suffering on my way to the bottom
I was falling deeper in midst of life crises.
Like a broken ship on a frozen island
Far from the seashore in the distant of the mind
Do you ever think of me the way I think of you?
Time is slipping away, and thoughts will never meet again.
Do you ever wonder why I do the things I do?
I guess you can guess by now.
I have been fooling myself, but that was miles back.
Eighty-six thousand four hundred seconds ago
I am not the same anymore.
Last night was the coldest night of my life.
Living a lie, I cannot live with it any longer.
I have been thinking about your decision.

And the attitude you took, I understand.
You know, there are a couple of things.
We need to go over and talk about
No, scratch that; forget about it.
I am just having a weak moment.
I am over it already, I hear you screaming out.
Unhappiness had a low point, and you have reached it.
I am struggling behind your thoughts.
I am sinking lower than anyone can imagine.
I am still standing in the rain, sinking fast.
I am a sinking mess, a drunkard stupidity.
I have troubles that are worrying me to death.
I hear my heart beating in my chest.
I did not sleep well with it pounding like that.
Is my mind telling me I am an emotional wreck?
I am going into shock acting a little crazy.
I believed in you went the tides were rolling in.
And your ship was sinking.
When you said you would love me forever
That was a beautiful lie,
I swallow your words hook, line and sinker.
I ingested your every thought.
I was not wise enough to know the difference.
I did not think I needed to
I was foolish enough to love you.
You were not happy with me you broke my heart.
With your beautiful lies

I was holding on to what you said.
Now I understand I was a fool.
Not seeing the handwriting on the wall
That is twenty-twenty now.
I am getting over you the hard way.
There is something I keep putting up with
This is not easy to explain to the heart.
I am struggling to let go of you.
My body is shifting into overdrive.
And it is coming out of me in fire.
I am burning up from the inside.
In the heat of the moment
That was the wrong thing to do.
You went about it the wrong way.
You did not want me inside your world.
So, you excused yourself.
I know you feel the vibe.
I am tired of looking over my shoulders.
Waiting on your respond

I WAITED ON YOU.

I waited for you until the end of the day.
Until the sun was slowly going down
Until the morning came again
I still waited, then my eyes filled with tears.
I waited until the storm passed.
I saw the seashore rushing back out to sea.
Like a hurricane twisted by a tornado
I was feeling insecure.
Clouds were bursting in midair.
Tears flowing like a river.
You can tell by the picture above.
I was filling up the sea.
I thought you would come for me.
But you never did.
You know what causes me to cry?
You have my heart and help complete me.

Loving you is suitable for me.
You are my redeeming quality.
When you are not blessing me
I cry about it; I did something wrong.
I have trouble living without your mercy.
I have trouble dealing with the madness.
I realize this is not me.
I am a sinking ship in shadow water.
Just deep enough not to make it to shore
Not far enough out to throw a lifeline to
A fast-sinking heart full of hope
Sleeping at the steering wheel
Running off the road, going over the edge
Waiting for you to come to my rescue?
I have been through so much.
I am doing everything in my power.
To keep it under control
Sometimes, I wonder why I am hesitating.
I am only human.
I feel forgotten. I must forgive myself.
Do this means living on edge of hopelessness.
Not making it into heaven.
Will I let my mistake blot me out?
I am riding high like a ghost rider.
I see you all over me, taking me under
I remember my first blessing.
I remember my first rescue,

There were times I could not breathe.
I felt betrayed by you, I had separate thoughts.
I have been breathless without you.
It is four in the morning,
I am trying to get you off my mind.
My future is dim, I am still crying about yesterday,
But I am hanging on from a broken cloud.
Tears became my best friend.
You became my provider.
I had trouble recovering.
And hope you are feeling the same.
All these feelings inside of me
Are struggles behind memories?
I see both of us in the mirror, smiling.
One moment later, It just me
I needed to try something new.
But I am mad with you and at you.
For walking away like you did
That was the hardest thing I had to face.
You left me feeling defenseless.
On common ground, I never felt so alone
You left a note saying nothing, but I am sorry.
It is better to have and need.
Than to need and not have
You have melted so deep into my skin.
That I cannot sleep without you.
So far, I have felt to keep you out.

I have loved you for too long.
Just to turn my back and walk away.
I do not want to feel or sound selfish.
But my scars are not healing.
Squiggling in the wheel well of life
Slowly dying outside human shell
I cannot leave my life in someone else's hands.
I got to get this out front and out of my head.
I would be unhappy without you.
I would give up and die; I am just fronting.
I am in this empty room looking for myself.
Like open space in the hallway of time
I have so much love for you
I am looking for that peace of mind.
I do not believe in rejection.
Those passages are all misunderstood.
I could have done better, I must admit.
Like a fool, I held on to the past too long.
I am sitting here alone, dealing with my emotions.
I thought our love would be everlasting.
I saw no need to worry, no need to be weary.
About what could have been?
The Lord knows this is not good for me.
The changing season has been messing with my head.
Living without you would truly tear my heart apart.
It had been years since I have been without love.
Waking up to emptiness

I cannot see any good years left in front of me.
I feel like a sinking heart.
It is nice to know there is resistance.
But my grasp is letting me down slowly.
I pray to overcome by sinking heart.
And find that someone who smiles is not against me.
I see hours of the morning without the sun flashing.
A heartbeat inside these walls is beating like a hiding secret.
I feel different about the way things are.
Like rain pouring out of me like broken tears
Falling from heaven window like raindrops
All over, around, and through me
Love understood my hurt and pain.
I need a helping hand. I believe the Lord can.
I need you to understand.
I am living for the love of you.
I am going to love you back.
And stand by you through thick and thin.
Life is good I am going to reflect that back to you.
Love continues to treat me so kindly.
I expected to love you forever.
I am a living example of what love should be.
What causes a heart to look like me?
I know you have heard all this before.
Loving you is coming back alive.
The best things are yet to come.
Holding on is the cure.

We shared good times in one place.
I hate I cannot borrow from tomorrow.
I would keep this love rolling in real-time.
You kept my heart beating.
We were always by each other's side.
I was a broken vessel in factual pieces.
I feel mistreated and not glued together.
Feeling alone and uncoordinated
Yet treated like someone you wanted.
Life is full of gifts and tithes.
Always good to give and receive.
There is nothing wrong with that.
I just do not have it in me anymore.
Life is not about getting even.
Time has its time slot for that.
You can be the cause of it all.
You can tell what sin been up to
A day ago, is still hurting like before.
Eyes act like knobs on your heart
That slowly turns but never unlocks.
Like windows of the soul looking out
You cannot see with your eyes closed.
Broken since yesterday in need of repair.
I know I hurt you, and I cannot live without you.
I keep an open mind and an honored face to be with you.
I am keeping it real; my heart is revealing what it feels.
Can I come to you if I feel unsafe?

I believed my heart would open and heal.
To exhale where I can breathe again.
I gathered up all my scattered pieces.
Like a zig saw puzzle without a picture
My life never felt reusable or redeemable.
I deserve another chance.
My life is an open book, like a child's story.
Dropping lines of love no longer covered
I had my share of difficulties.
I had good days and bad days.
I had no act right but trying to get right.
Understanding this took me awhile.
I had to fight to edit my life.
I had to change things.
To stop acting like I use to
Love is not a book on the shelf that you cannot share.
Love is not selfish.
You cannot sit down on love.
The cornerstone that holds me together is you.
I found enough room to forgive and love again.
Mistakes of my past are haunting me.
The time came for me; please forgive me.
I want to get in my car and drive all night.
Turn off my telephone and listen to the radio.
I do not need to hear your voice in my head.
You have always been my setback.
Thinking of your hugs and loves and kisses.

I am trying to fight through that to live again.
I am not trying to let you go,
I want to get to know you better.
I wanted to experience something new.
Create a whole new world for us.
After seventy-four years plus one
I should have known better.
I pray that my favorite song works.
For a moment
I forgot that we had sung together.
Like day-of-old, I miss you.
You were my favorite song to sing.
Yesterday looks like a day ago.
I wanted so much out of life.
But I was living without a dream.
I thought you were born to help me.
I woke up thinking about you.
Calling your name out of my sleep
I promise I thought it was you and me.
I was not trying to do anything different.
Nothing will be the same without you.
Playing these stupid games
Standing around playing in the cold
Standing in an open field counting raindrops
Thinking you are the star the Lord took from me.
The noise in the background is loud.
But I am not willing to sacrifice.

Talking to myself and falling
I did not want you to leave.
Living without you is killing me.
I am afraid of the dark, standing in a locked room.
I am afraid of losing my soul.
I know you were my Happiness.
I do not want to end up alone.
As old saint in a mobile wheelchair
If I could live this crooked life over
There are things I would do better.
I would deal myself a better hand.
Not the one I am dealing with now.
I would keep you with me every day.
And thank the Lord for every moment.
You might be living a good life.
Not thinking otherwise
I have pictures that tell a different story.
I see my life through a telescope.
I see what my life could have been.
So many yesterdays had gone by.
Like water under a bridge
My experiences and behaviors reflected that.
Now I am crying like a baby.
About something I cannot do anything about,
I took a different approach and stood strong.
I look for another shoulder I could lean on
I prayed that my wounds would heal.

That my pain and heartaches would subside
I hurt so bad that I let time slip away.
Trying to steal time back but feeling locked out.
What I lost is on the backside of forever.
Like fading memories losing its grip
Living excuses will put a hold on your heart.
False love will cause you to struggle and not breathe.
Love sure is energy that fuels the heart.
At any given moment, life can go up in smoke.
And the shame on your face will tell the story.
And you still can come up short.
Leaving the past behind is a good step.
Somewhere along the road, your head cleared.
You move your heart by keeping it alive.
Letting go of the past can help you move forward.
I knew then that the Lord had stepped in.
My mind was out of time, and he knew that.
Heart and soul were lining up to fall.
I saw the handwriting on the wall.
Afraid of losing what I work so hard for
Searching for that peace of mind that eludes me.
I wanted to enjoy life and live it fully.
I saw life hiding behind blind eyes.
I was living under two shades of darkness.
I was living life with regrets.
I am in the process of correcting that.
My shamelessness went on and on.

Now that I am a day older and much wiser.
What is a man to do besides moving on?
When all he had said and done had not materialize
It would be much wiser and better to let go.
There are no more avenues to take or travel.
When judgment day is next in line
And the Lord says you stop trying,
What do you do when it is too late?
Where are you going from here?
When words are spoke against you
And they cut so deep that you bleed out.
Do not let your biggest mistake.
Continue to grow and consume you.
You can be so far out there.
That you can lose control
And never get back home
The end can be nearer than you think.
You just wanted to be free and love again.
When divorce had the final word
There is something wrong when love still hurts.
You must accept that and move on
Learn from a Sinking Heart
That love and time can mend a broken heart.
Love and grip are a cord that binds a sinking heart.
Where our past and present speak
About never-ending love

BROKEN WITH LOVE
Getting Through Your Emotions

IF I HAD YOU?

If I had you, I would stop dreaming of perfection.
Nothing else would have my attention,
I would keep smiling without the sun shining.
Valleys would not be deep enough or wide enough.
To keep me from you
High wind and thunderstorms would not hold me back.
If I had you, I would stop dreaming of perfection.
Nothing else would matter; you would be my shining star.
I would stay afloat forever; you would be my purpose.
I would keep going on and on; my love for you would be endless.
I will never stop sharing my love with you.
Because you are perfect for me,
I would conquer my darkest fears.
My life would be perfect loving you.
My love for you would be more than a thought.
That would fit perfectly in my heart.
I will keep showering you with love.
Until the end come for us both
I pray it will be at the same time.
My life would be a struggle to live without you.
Our love will be more than energy or light.
Never grow dim and never burn out.
For each sparkle would light up the night
The Lord would see the desires of our heart.
With never-ending fire and desire

You have become the key to my heart.
That moment that I been living for
You have melted away all my coldness.
Your touch took away any pain.
That I may have been feeling.
You are the secret to my beginning.
You have that touch that very soul search for
Filling their heart with true and divine love
Putting hope in tomorrow otherwise would never be so.
A thousand years from now, they will talk about us.
In a different world, In another language,
Others will experience.
What we are feeling now.
I feel no other love like ours
No blue skies but yours, No touches but yours
No hugs but yours, No love but yours, no kisses but yours.
That is why I admire everything about you.
And my life became so sweet.
In ten thousand words and the person I became,
Is because of the love you gave.
You are the one thing that keeps my heart beating.

Besides Loving You Forever

I see the moon in the arms of the stars.
Dancing against the blue skies
With all of space and time, watching
All eyes in heaven are excited.
Besides loving you forever
Nothing else matters to me
My heart is free only to love thee.
The wind cannot blow my love out, of course.
I feel the sun rays touching my skin.
Warming every part of me
While I am thinking of thee
My heart beats with endless desire
Besides loving you forever
I would not have it any other way.
I would swim the Seven Seas for your love.
Carry the world on my shoulders.
I would be a powerlifter,
I will keep lifting you higher and higher.
Be there for you twenty-four-seven.
Always and forever
My love for you is like the stars above.
Like the background of heaven, endless
Until space and time became one
My world would be all about you.
Besides loving you forever
My love will never know an ending.

I will love you across time and back again.
Where the soul will live forever
And the sea will have a new beginning.
From all equal and unequal points
I am giving you all of me and how I feel right now.
Loving you forever is not long enough.
That is why I will live this life forever.
Where I can love you always
I understand why clouds sometime cry.
Why tear drip like the morning dew
And rainbows remind me of a promise.
Lingering with sweetest of love
As the stars lifted their eyes to heaven
I see the morning clouds filled with tears.
I would cry too if I awaken without you.

Missing you like yesterday.

I am about to pour me a glass of wine.
Sit by the fireplace and kicked up my heels.
Think about what I miss when I let you go.
I have been turning and twisting in my sleep.
I am missing you like never before.
I am updating my love for you.
I have been thinking about you lately.
My love, my heart, that voice in my head
Asking why you are doing this to yourself.
That touch that you are feeling was once real.
I am thinking about you reaching into heaven.
I am going crazy thinking about you all day.
I am struggling with my emotions.
The very things that alive inside of me
We reached into heaven and found each other.
Our love for each other is sweeter than honey.
A love I never thought would never be.
A dream I never thought would come true.
I never thought I would stop hurting.
You collected my scattered dreams.
Making it possible for me to live again.
I know you have read this a thousand times by now.
Your love is still real to me in every viable way.
Every part of you is touching me under my skin.
An itch I cannot reach or scratch.
Only the Lord knows what is going on with me.

Ever since the moment we touch.
I have been reaching all my life to fill this empty space.
Nothing has been the same for me since
You gave life to my dying soul.
Like flowing electricity around a circuit
I have grown in my love for you.
That each wave brings about a new beat
That keeps going on and on
I will still feel the same about you a thousand light years from now.
Yesterday came and gone, I am still here for you.
I am missing you like yesterday always and forever pass tomorrow.
As each ship sails, I will be your captain on a sinking ship.
I will hold you up until the life in me is gone.
We have touched the sky, and the rest has faded away.
My life, my heart is open to love you forevermore.
On this side of heaven until the Lord call me home.

JUST A THREAD

In the middle of a field
Next to a fence that is leaning.
I trusted my heart.
When it told me that you love me.
I trust my heart when my ears hear.
Those words that flowed from your lips.
Your words where strong but, at the same time, weak
I never thought this would hurt the way it does.
It has been spring, and summer is pushing to an end.
Fall is days before winter, and it will be cold.
What is in front of you still hurts?
The Lord is not going to let you fall.
He knows you been fighting against the odds.
That trouble is not going to let you go.
Sin is not a gentleman.
Sin is just a thread that is trying to hold you down.
Sin wants you to bend, to see your life end.
Life seemed like an impossible task to complete.
While the handwriting on the wall is clear
Sin will make it hard for you to survive it.
Sin is not going to give up; evil is not going to give in
You can let the past go and live again.
Let the storm pass, and be real to yourself.
If the Lord can turn water into wine
Just think how much more he can do for you.
There is nothing that can keep him from loving you.

If he can heal the sick and give sight to the blind
Just think how much more he can do for you.
There should be no doubt about your faith.
You can stop crying in the midnight hours.
And stop judging others for their shortfalls.
You have faults that look like theirs
You have been in an analogous situation.
You want the Lord faith to hold you.
Lift you off the ground and sustain you.
Place you on higher ground, overlooking your troubles.
You want to stop looking back and holding out.
You want to break down walls and live again.
You know how to fix me, my Lord.
You know what to do to fix me.
Sin was looking for me to stay down.
I am refusing to live how I used to be.

The Lord Gave Me the Strength

The Lord gave me the strength.
He picked me up; He did not hold me down.
He kept me holding on; He did not stop there.
I did not give up; I kept reaching out.
So many good things came my way.
I had to run and tell somebody.
The Lord gave me the strength.
Every day, in every way
I never understood clearly.
I cannot wait to see His face.
My shout will not be long enough.
My praise will not be that great
But it will be all that I have to give.
The Lord gave me the strength to run this race.
Let me walk back down memory lane.
When I kept coming up short
His love for me was constant.
Let me tell you another memory.
When I was feeling incomplete
He came to my rescue and renewal me.
All I needed was Him.
You gave me the strength to run this race.
I am so thankful for that.
He saw something in me.

That I did not see in myself
You gave me words that encourage me.
Like, I can do this. Just hold on and never stop trying.
You came this far by faith; do not give up now.
I know there were times you were crying.
I had your back on that one, too.
The Lord knew you were trying.
To get to the other side
You saw your faith was strong.
And you were willing to hang on.
He built a bridge across troubled water.
He knew you could not swim.
That you would drown
He became your life support.
He is my shelter in stormy weather.
He gave you the strength to be strong.
Now, I am walking across dry ground.

The Inspiration of Love
Having Someone to Love You

Dreams and Roses are one.

Dreams and Roses are one.
In my dreams, I had so much fun
The roses of my garden became.
The flower of my love that I felt for you.
They both come from nothing to be something.
I noticed a rose growing on the side of a hill.
With pieces of thoughts turning into dreams
I felt the wind blowing against my skin.
This rose had a dream of coming from the dust.
I could not read the rose mind.
But it was reaching for heaven.
The mower kept cutting it down.
I understood it pain.
Like the voice of harsh words
Coming from a person that you love
The rose had a dream to be something.
More than a beautiful flower
Waking up with the sun shining in its face
The rose wanted to grab the sun and pull it down.
And wake up each morning with a smile.
Warming hearts like yours and mines
Giving each moment its own chance to love
It brought back memories of you, and I
How we first started and still are.
With memories keeping our dreams alive
We cherished every minute being each other's rose.

Sometimes, we push each other aside.
But we keep our eyes on the sparrow.
Because our love is a garden of love
Knowing at the end of the day, our love will be.
In rays of sun beaming to rise
We sawed the world before it was.
And we lived inside this world below the earth's crust.
We would smile at each other below the surface.
As we pushed upward through the soil
Before the sun grew dim and stopped shining
We grew healthier and more beautiful with time.
Loving the vision with the morning dew,
Our tears wept in our eyes with sweetness.
Each glimpse from the morning bud
Our love came closer to the shore.
We would reach for the light.
Our passion had climbed from the walls of despair.
And there, we supported each other.
Awakened by the rays of the sun, we became one.
Our petals opened with a flow of energy.
And we pushed toward the open sky.
Where the beauty of God's Divine love is present
We were there for each other as the morning rose.
We would reach our potential, for we were above the surface.
For the world was ours, and our love was deeply rooted.

We shared so much love between us, and it grew like wildfire
For we were each other's rose in another dimension.
To be each other's rose behind each other dreams

So Much Love Between Us

There is so much love between us
The Lord would be proud, for we've tried so hard
To mend our broken hearts
Though our love is healing
We deserve a chance to love again.
Like a fractured arm mending
Our hearts, yours, and mine
Will stand the test of time.
We thought we would be over each other by now.
In this empty room, I feel tears flowing.
To wash away the hurt that we once felt
Let us give love a chance to breathe again.
Then our hearts have the right to live once more
I cannot breathe when I am away from you.
You are the oxygen that keeps me breathing.
We both hurt in places that seem unbearable.
Our hearts are trying to make sense of it all.
Darkness is dressing up like a light.
I pray and hope we are not fooling ourselves.
The only thing I feel and see is you?
I never thought it would come to this.
Trying to find excuses because.
We are living without each other.
Living in separate worlds
I cannot see myself without you.
If it takes everything in me, I will keep living for you.

There is no other I can love better.
My love for you is about being real.
More precious than anything, and I cherish you.
I thought we believed in each other.
Without you, I would surely die.
Without you, nothing exists.
I would like to think you are my reason for living.
Your love is safe with me.
We both are broke
We both still carry our hurt around.
Parts of our hearts even bleed.
Our fear is our tears, and we keep weeping.
There is so much love between us
That we need each other; we are each other's light

Un-Substituted Love

A heart can cry.
Like a missing rose on a stem.
As my passion for you grows
As deep as any river that flows,
As high as the sky may go.
There is no end or limit insight,
For my love for you is endless.
There are unfamiliar places loves can grow.
As sweet as a honey cone,
One place is my heart.
You will always be my number one.
There is none as sweet as thee.
Let love belong to the palm of the heart.
Where winter is next in line behind fall
Having that holy passion for you,
I only dare to dream.
How pure my love is,
That flows like milk and honey.
Across the open sky,
With each thought of thee
My heart sings with incredible songs of love,
You are near; I can feel your presence.
Knowing that your presence is good for me
And your absence will hurt from the bottom up,
I searched the world over.
My heart will never stop exploring,

No matter what I am going through,
What I feel for you is true
I know what I have in you.
It will never grow old.
I love the way you make me strong.
Your touch will never be my coldness
I feel so close to you.

Reconnecting
Creating a New Love

O TELL ME, MY BELOVED,

It was you that captured my heart.
With your touch, I was set free.
Our first walk together
I poured out my heart to you.
It was obvious how I felt about you.
Our first kiss seals against my heart
My lips still sizzle to this day.
Your smile always warms my heart.
And create unforgettable thoughts.
O tell me, my beloved.
O tell me, my beloved
Where have the years I have been missing gone?
The years of loving you have not left me.
As the leaves falling from a tree
Reflection a change in the season
But never a difference in my heart
O tell me, my beloved,
O tell me, my beloved
Where have the years I missed you faded to?
Embrace me; my love holds me.
Let us remember yesteryears.
Our love will never grow old or cold.
O tell me, my beloved; O tell me, my dear,
Those years that left me, where are they?
My heart still coils from your touch.
O tell me, my beloved

How have I been living this long?
There is no me without you.
Like dripping rain from the clouds
In the distance afar, my rainforest
I know why heaven is crying.
When the storms of life roll in
Undying love comforted me.
for I know you are a part of me
We still have so much to share.
Love still runs through our veins.
Like a warm blanket, I feel you.
We warm each other with a hug.
God gave us love for each other.
All my life, you have been a keeper.
Every day that passed by me.
It been deeper.
O tell me, my beloved, my beloved
Do you have the answer?

AND SHE SPOKE.

Like a thousand dreams
Like a broken bed,
I cannot lie to myself anymore.
How can I say good-bye?
Without letting go or losing a part of me
Why, then, after all these years
My heart still beats for you.
I keep loving you and feeling the same.
Years of my life had passed by.
Years have passed that I cannot get back.
I cannot think or breathe without you.
I loved you when the wind was young.
I loved you in my youth.
Now that I am old and gray.
Nothing about my heartbeat had changed.
I still feel the same about you.
As yesterday is still in the past
I kept hope alive in my eyes.
I kept seeing you in my dreams.
And you are loving me the same.
I never gave up my dream.
I knew you were the one.
That would complete my thoughts.
Help form the words of my lips.
From the first word I spoke
From the first time, I set eyes on you

All those years ago,
I remember everyone.
The first step, the first look,
I counted them all.
The long, the short, all the ones in between
I still hold those memories.
All the years I loved you.
Morning, noon, and all day
My heart still races, My palm still sweats.
Just the thought of you
Just the touch of you
After all these years
I still feel the same about you,
That you feel about me

A Thousand Kisses

A thousand kisses plus one
A million sweet hugs, sweet as a honeybee
Sounding like a songbird, whispering
From the ocean floor, free like the air
Breezing through my lungs
Hissing the waves of songs
Sounding forever so sweet
Sounding like a hummingbird
Flying free through open space
I think the Lord for you.
My love will always be for you and always.
A thousand kisses plus one
Like a thousand hugs
Knowing that I love you.
Is desire rushing through my heart?
A thousand kisses plus one
A thousand touches plus mine
One squeeze, one hug, one love
Embracing the quiet of my heart
I can feel you,
I have a fear of living without you.
I thought Happiness was impossible.
I talked about it and believed it.
Look what the Lord did for me.
You walked into my life.
Blessing me with a piece of heaven

I will be the love you can count on
A thousand kisses plus one
Like a never-ending hug
Thousand times over
Wrapped around my heart.
Dressed in a blanket of love.
I know the Lord has been good to me.
I have you to love.
I will love you always.
Nothing less than a thousand years from now
Loving you with unspeakable joy
The depth of my love, is you?
A thousand kisses plus

Relationships
Growing In Love

Excellent Times between Us

Excellent times between us were pictures perfect for love.
And everything between us is exciting.
I keep looking and seeing you.
But I am slowly falling under your smell.
My smiles keep coming back empty.
The years between us were too much.
Years, I did not want to give up.
There were times I looked back and smiled.
Sometimes, I just think aloud.
Praying this is not a dream.
I wish I could turn back the hands of time.
I would go back to my fortieth birthday,
I see no need to go back any further
It was two years ago that I met you.
Since then, we have had good times.
You put new steps in an older man's walk.
You put new sparks in an older man's heart.
When I look into your eyes
I can see stars around heaven dancing.
Good times and all, and no end in sight
Times between us were good times, always.
Times between us were one after another.
Times between us were one of a kind.
Times between us were never a waste.
Good times between us were always good.
The year she was born, so was my child.

Here I am, holding a woman half my age.
I knew it was not going to last.
She was my wish upon a falling star.
And the Lord knew my heart.
I was two generations two early.
Life had never been so good until I found her.
I see the young woman in her.
But I see the older man in me.
There is something about her.
That makes a grown mancry.
Now I understand why.
Why men wish on a falling star?
Why they die trying to be young,
Wishing for younger days
Trying to hold on to excellent times.

The Lord, Feel your shame.

I know you feel ashamed.
The hurt in your eyes is screaming.
I know it hurts, but I have her now.
You mistreated her under your roof.
I will not treat her the same.
I see so many mistakes.
You took full advantage of
I will not have her reliving tears.
Crying behind broken promises
I will be by her side.
Treat her like the queen she is.
I will not have her living your mistakes.
I will not take her thoughts for granted.
I will not treat her like you did yesterday.
I will put her first and keep her there.
Become a great provider for her.
Let me put this to your mind.
The Lord feels your shame.
There is no next time for you.
There is no reason.
For sin to come around again
And if it done, you have a soldier on your side
There is no reason for you to cry anymore.
We both know you are good at faking it.
You tried that before; it did not work out for you.
Your time is up

I want you to know, hear it from me.
I am speaking for her.
Listen: no phone calls, no texting
Listen: no Instagram,
No more Facebook or
Any connecting thread, nothing like that
I am the muscle, standing guard.
With an attitude, warning not to cross the line.
I can be an evil bulldog,
A lion in the jungle
I am a one-person woman.
She is my queen. Do you get the message sin?
Do not cross me or mess with my salvation.
You will have no reason to deal with me.
I know you feel ashamed. Let us keep it real.
Just walk away.
Looking back can turn you into a stone.

I Will Love You Always

You are looking good today, as always.
I will love you through time; now and forevermore.
I love the way you wear your hair.
You know I love you all the days of the week.
There is not a day I do not think about you.
There is nothing better than 24/7
I will love you always and forever.
My heart is touching and agreeing.
I am better because of you.
I can see tomorrow in your eyes.
All because of you, I can breathe again.
Before you, I was a lost man without a dream.
You gave me a reason to believe in heaven.
Moving without you would be difficult.
Nothing about you is getting old.
We are best friends to each other.
Life and living revolves around us.
We are the reason life is.
You are my best friend; I am yours
You are my ebony eyes,
My sweet chocolate lollipop
Sometimes I wake up from my dreams.
And smile, for I know I have a piece of heaven.
You know, love comes in so many colors.
You are a rainbow pouring over me.
You have a unique way of showing it.

You are my heavenly rain dripping honeydew
My heart is feeling every minute of you.
You are my world, my life, my beginning.
And I never what this to come to an ending.
What and where would I be without you
If I ever forget to tell you
If I lose my voice, I will write it down.
If I ever misspell your name
I will write it down a thousand times.
I want you to know I will love you forever.
And what I feel is so into you.

Inside Forgiveness

Inside forgiveness, I forgave.
Do you remember what you once were?
You stopped me in my tracks; loving you became secondary.
Blessings stopped flowing; you could have helped me out.
Because I was holding onto worldly things
I was refusing to let see it for what it is.
Now, you want to blame me for your shortcomings.
You could have found anyone else to talk to
That you could complain to that would help you through
You found yourself begging to make things clear.
But no one was listening to you.
You are not a mile from where you once were.
Drifting on memories, trying to let go.
It is sad to think you came this far to give in
On the corner of love and hate without a new beginning
What you thought was impossible.
You felt like you were going crazy.
You never thought healing would take place.
You never thought mending would be.
You were feeling powerless and insecure.
Trying to use words to say what you felt.
You could not find the right one.
Time will tell if you got it together.
Or you are just another week vessel.
You still discovered that love does hurt.

Especially when you are in love alone and you feel empty.
Inside forgiveness, I forgave.
I thank the Lord for seeing something in me.
That I did not see an opportunity in
I thank the Lord for visiting with me.
I knew I had faults that were out of limit.
Awaking each day to face another moment of the same.
Inside forgiveness, I forgave.
It feels wonderful blessed.
Inside forgiveness, I forgave.
Love helps me to see and know.
Inside forgiveness, I forgave.
Giving me a handup to help my heart grow up.
Looking beyond others faults and see mine

A Love I Can Believe In

I am sitting here thinking.
How I should deal with my feels
With my life going in circle
We can agree that what is between us is real.
We have love, we can believe in
That we can share true love and not give in
With our heart, soul, and mind
On the same page, we can agree to turn together.
Love that I can trust will hold me.
When trouble stacked against me
Love that makes me smile when I am sad.
When I get old and gray, I can still laugh.
I believe love can abide and stay strong.
Between us, when things are going the wrong way
I can still smile and stand still.
And believe in what we have.
There is something I do not need from love.
What I do not need is love that will fade away
I need love that will last in rough times.
Be a shoulder I can lean on
I need a love that will be there for me.
That is not willing to substitute for the real thing.
I do not need a love that is trying to act real.
I need a love that will stand up and be count
That is not going to run and hide, bend or fold.
I do not need love.

That is going to beat me up with words.
And never have anything nice to say.
I do not need a love that is all about self.
I do not need a love that is full of itself.
I need a love that is going to shower me.
I need love I can believe in,
Love that knows my name and believe in my dreams.
I need a love that can crawl.
Out of valleys and climb mountains.
Be shoulder I can stand on and depend on
When I am crying
Be a hand that wiped my weeping eyes.
I need a love that will not give up on me.
Because I am going through difficulties
I need a love that will see me in a dark place.
reach for me and be my beaming light.
Be a love in which I can believe.

My Morning Dew

Heaven woke up this morning.
And looked out and saw me.
Having a conversation with a star
My eyes were closed, and heaven said.
I see inside your heart, I know.
You are smiling like never before.
All the love you came to know.
Tears from your eyes, I see.
I will call morning dew, after you
For her
All your hugs and kisses are deep and more profound
Like morning dew hanging on a silver leaf
From your smile, the morning dew came to be
Your sweet lips remind me how perfect a smile can be.
Your love is as beautiful as the heart I held so close.
It is like waking up with heaven next to you.
A thousand dreams in one, my love for you
It is all true; I woke up in heaven.
In the arms of the morning dew
Your lips were sweeter than a honeycomb.
As if the Lord reserved this moment just for me.
My name, my address, my number, he knew.
Your lips touched me like the morning dew.
To Him
Embracing me with love like the morning sun
Breaking through my heart from a touch above

Like a careless whisper dancing on an ocean floor
In the morning, with morning dew
I will always and only feel you.
All the places my life's journey has taken me.
I found words falling off my lips.
Like morning dew, in touch, in a hug, in a kiss
Standing at the edge of night
With a painted picture of heaven
All I could see was you.
My morning dew.
All the millions of ways to experience Happiness.
They are all rolled up in you.
From this moment on, heaven will smile.
Because you gave morning dew a reason to be
Every time the sun sets and rises.
My love will be that spark that comes from below and above.
Like morning dew that go and come
Both
When I look into your eyes
I can see and feel stars come alive.
Dancing like sparkling butterflies in season
It is like reaching out and catching a star.
None as beautiful as your morning dew
None more beautiful than each morning with you
Like honey in the sweetness of the morning
I stand here in awe.

Praying that my morning will never end.
For my smile is from loving you
My morning dew.
I never thought a broken heart would heal.
Until I tasted your morning love
The love that you gave was so pure.
Because of you, I can live again.
If I could line up all the stars
I would never get to the end of them.
That is the only way I would have it.
I will never stop loving thee.
You touch me, and I am here for you.
You unlock the melody of my heart.
I sing with the joy of your love.
Key and reason I love
My morning dew.
I am not asking for much.
Just to love you forever.
Like the morning before each day
Heaven is not quiet. I can see.
A hand wiping the tears from my eyes.
Like morning dew, all my mornings before
I marvel at your beauty, my morning dew

Last Thoughts

God's love and kindness have never stopped amazing me. I can swim the seven seas and paddle across the deepest part of the ocean and come to the end of my life and still love the Lord the same as the first day He saved me, for He had been my life: My Everything, My Beginning and My Ending.

1 Corinthians 13:4-5=Love is
Isaiah 41:10= strength in you
Exodus 15:2= Giving Song and Victory

www.ingramcontent.com/pod-product-compliance
Lightning Source LLC
Chambersburg PA
CBHW050249010526
44107CB00003B/251